For information address:

SAGE PUBLICATIONS, INC.
275 South Beverly Drive
Beverly Hills, California 90212

SAGE PUBLICATIONS LTD
St George's House / 44 Hatton Garden
London EC1N 8ER

International Standard Book Number 0-8039-0755-9

Library of Congress Catalog Card No. L.C. 76-47117

FIRST PRINTING

When citing a Research Paper, please use the proper form. Remember to cite the series title and include the paper number. One of the two following formats can be adapted (depending on the style manual used):

(1) LANTZ, H. R. (1976) "Marital Incompatibility and Social Change in Early America." Sage Research Papers in the Social Sciences (Studies of Marriage and the Family Series, No. 90-026) Beverly Hills and London: Sage Publications.

OR

(2) Lantz, Herman R. 1976. *Marital Incompatibility and Social Change in Early America.* Sage Research Papers in the Social Sciences, vol. 4, series no. 90-026 (Stud-ies of Marriage and the Family Series). Beverly Hills and London: Sage Publications.

WITHDRAWN

Contents

VOLUNTARILY CHILDLESS COUPLES:
The Emergence of a Variant Lifestyle

ELLEN MARA NASON
Sinclair Community College

MARGARET M. POLOMA
University of Akron

CHILDLESS COUPLES: SOME
PRELIMINARY CONSIDERATIONS

Throughout history the family has been an important—if not the most important—institution in society. The twentieth century, however, has witnessed some dramatic changes within the family, with the nuclear family beginning to generate variant patterns. Highly individualized and industrialized society has permitted the emergence of a variety of family forms, including dual-work families where both husband and wife are gainfully employed outside the home, single-parent families of either mother-only or father-only, cohabitation without entering a marriage contract, and diverse type of communal families. Undoubtedly, even with wide variations among and within such family types, reproduction and socialization of children continues to be an important task that renders their fitting into a broad definition of "family."

Modern technology has made possible the voluntary choice of another form of marriage that some writers are reluctant to term "family"—namely, childfree marriages. Rodgers (1973: 26) in discussing the reproductive function of the family notes:

> As a matter of fact, the term typically applied to a married pair without children is more likely to be *couple* than it is to be *family*. Having children, not simply being married, becomes the significant criterion for qualifying a family. Couples who find they are biologically incapable of having children also feel pressures placed upon them to adopt children to attain family status. There is a quality of evaluation toward childless couples which implies they have not totally fulfilled themselves until they have reproduced.

Childfree marriages—whether they be acknowledged as "families" or not—may be increasing in this final quarter of the twentieth century. No question, childless marriages have always existed, but they have been viewed as a curse rather than as a blessing. The Biblical accounts of Sarah and Abraham of the Old Testament as well as Elizabeth and Zechariah in the New Testament give evidence of the joy that both couples experienced with the birth of a first child late in their lives. This same stress on the importance of childbearing may be found among cultures where biological illegitimacy is not problematic but barrenness is, or where failure to bear a child is grounds for divorce. The need for a high fertility rate coupled with less than efficient methods of birth control had made childbearing a norm form which few desired to deviate. Undoubtedly childless marriages of an earlier era were almost universally *involuntarily* childless.

The twentieth century, however, has witnessed a drastic increase in world population and has provided the technology to control fertility. Not only has much involuntary childlessness been reduced through medical developments, but voluntary childfreeness is possible due to improved contraceptives, sterilization techniques, and legalized abortion. It appears safe to assert that the rise of childlessness among educated middle-class couples is due to voluntary action rather than involuntary sterility.

TRENDS IN CHILDLESSNESS: A REVIEW OF CENSUS DATA

The phenomenon of voluntary childlessness has received only the passing attention of family sociologists as evidenced by the treatment of the topic in family texts bearing copyrights of the 1970s. Martinson (1970), for example, comments that marriages that are childness by choice are practically nonexistent. Duvall (1971) refers to voluntary childlessness as a "rare married couple who chooses to have no children at all." Leslie (1973) includes childlessness as one of the "pathologies associated with family life" indicative of "rampant individualism." Bell (1971) does engage in a brief discussion of the childfree way of life, but he fails to distinguish between those who are voluntarily and involuntarily childless.

The existence of childless couples has been recognized by those who are familiar with demographic analysis. In addition to the data provided by the U.S. Bureau of the Census (1973), articles focusing on the demographic facts of childlessness include Grabill and Glick (1958); Whelpton, et al. (1966); Kiser, et al. (1968); Freedman, et al. (1969); Sklar (1971); Veevers (1971); and Rao (1974). These articles point to the fact that childlessness appears to be declining, presumably due to a decrease in the number of *involuntarily* childless couples. However, in a more recent analysis

Grindstaff (1976) contends that the rates of childlessness for both blacks and whites have increased—for whites since 1960 and for blacks since 1969. He suggests that this trend may continue in the future due to later age at marriage, completed family size occurring at younger ages, improved contraception, legal abortion, temporary postponement becoming permanent postponement, and pressures of population growth.

Comparison of the 1960 census figures with those of 1970 tends to support Grindstaff's projection for the future. As Table 1 indicates, there is some increase in the percent of childless married women under 30 years of age, but a decrease in childlessness for women over 30. While there is an overall 2.2 percent increase in childlessness among married women of childbearing age from the 1960 to the 1970 census, it is not clear whether a greater percentage of women are postponing childbearing *or* whether they are opting for a childfree state.

There are data to suggest that the attitudes toward childlessness are changing toward a greater acceptance of the right of the couple to opt for a childfree state. In comparing a 1965 sample of college students with a 1970 sample, Pohlman, et al. (1971) found a shift toward a greater tolerance of childless marriages. This shift was reported prior to the media coverage of a childfree alternative, including the appearance of Ellen Peck's *The Baby Trap* (1971), popular magazine and television coverage of childfree couples, an economic recession which may correlate with an increase in childlessness (as it did during the depression), as well as much concern about "shortages" that increase as our limited resources are consumed by an affluent population. Given the social situation of the 1970s, this change in attitude observed by Pohlman and his colleagues may become even greater and may be reflected in a behavior change as well as an attitude change.

POPULAR PRESENTATION OF A CHILDFREE ALTERNATIVE

Until recently the media's presentation of a childfree marriage as an alternative to a family with children was practically nonexistent. With the rise of feminism and increased opportunities for women, some women became more vocal about the desirability of remaining voluntarily childless. In one of the earlier articles on the subject, Gael Green (*Saturday Evening Post*, 1963) challenged the concept of mothering: "I don't want to have any children. Motherhood is only a part of marriage, and I am unwilling to sacrifice the other equally important feminine roles upon the over-exalted altar of parenthood." Her remark is re-echoed by Lynnel Michels in the popular women's magazine, *Redbook* (1970), and by sev-

TABLE 1
Percentage of Childless Married White Women,
15 Years of Age and Over, Ever Married, by Age
(Comparison of 1960 and 1970 Data)

	1960	1970	Percent Difference
Total	16.3%	15.9%	− .4%
15 to 44	14.6%	16.8%	2.2%
15 to 19	46.4%	53.7%	7.3%
20 to 24	25.0%	37.7%	12.7%
25 to 29	12.3%	16.1%	3.8%
30 to 34	9.6%	8.1%	− 1.5%
35 to 39	10.2%	7.0%	− 3.2%
40 to 44	13.0%	8.1%	− 4.9%
45 to 49	17.1%	10.1%	− 7.0%
50 to 54	19.9%	13.1%	− 6.8%
55 to 59	20.3%	16.8%	− 3.5%
60 to 64	18.6%	19.0%	.4%
65 and over	16.4%	17.0%	.6%

Source: Compiled from data presented in U.S. Bureau of the Census Subject Reports *Women by Number of Children Ever Born* from 1960 and 1970.

eral other journalists. Nigel Balchin, a noted English novelist, has also added his voice to what journalists seem to indicate is a steadily growing trend in recent years; that is, looking at parenthood and children as a conscious choice to be made by the married couple from several available roles. Balchin (1965: 10) contends:

[Children] are destructive of the emotional life of the average man. A man getting married may realize vaguely that he will one day have a family, and even desire it. What he certainly doesn't realize is the change in his relationship with his wife that the coming of children will involve . . . within a few months he finds he is now married to a mother.

Three nonresearch oriented books appeared on the topic of the childfree lifestyle in the 1970s. *The Baby Trap* (1971) by Peck was an attack on the media which, she contends, sells the concept of desiring children to a gullible public. Peck's argument basically revolves around the idea that once someone accepts the sales pitch of the media and is open to the "babysell" of manufacturers of children's items, the baby trap has been sprung and certain inevitable problems tend to arise; for example, spouses will not be as close as when first married, there will be less money, less personal freedom, and so forth.

Radl (1973), the mother of two children, attempts to offer to those who haven't yet had children rationales for considering a childfree alternative. "Any childless woman considering combining motherhood and a career should stop and determine which might mean more right now, before the biological facts are in." Radl is concerned not only about telling people they need not feel guilty about disliking parenthood, but also that people should examine their motives for wanting children. This work describes Radl's own personal experiences of parenthood; her frustrations in dealing with a series of conflicting roles. It, like Peck's effort, is aimed at a wife-only audience.

The Silvermans, also in 1971, attempted to present an argument against having children by approaching the topic from a negative viewpoint; that is, they present arguments designed to show "wrong" or negative reasons for parenthood. What the Silvermans, and to some extent Peck and Radl advocate is:

> Women and men should carefully analyze their motives for parenthood with the intention of determining: (1) if their desire to have children honestly reflects their own wishes or if it represents a sense of expectation or compulsion arising from sociocultural pressures; (2) if, already being parents, the birth of another child is truly necessary or advisable in terms of the best interests of their existing families and society in general; (3) if their motives for seeking parenthood are altruistic or selfish [Silverman, 1971: 38].

In other words, what these authors are advocating is freedom of choice about a subject people have not traditionally been in the habit of thinking of during previous decades: a choice concerned with the having or the not having of children.

While such presentations and discussions may be accused of over-statement of the case in stressing the problems of marriages with children and the bliss of a childfree state, they do perform the valuable function of providing an alternative model to couples. In reading such materials it becomes apparent that marriage and parenthood need not be synonymous terms—couples do have a choice to parent or not to parent.

The popular media has provided some limited information on the phenomenon of childfree couples, but systematic data collected by social scientists is less readily available. In view of our dynamic sociohistoric situation, which may be witnessing an increase in the number of voluntarily childfree couples, such marriages merit observation. While we have already cited some demographic articles dealing with this subject, recent social psychological studies which could help to describe childless marriages have been generally lacking. The existing literature does warrant consideration, however, in an attempt to determine what is already known about the subject and what questions remain to be answered.

SOCIAL SCIENCE RESEARCH ON CHILDLESSNESS

The higher incidence of childlessness during the Great Depression in the U.S. is reflected in the interest shown in the topic by some soical scientists in the 1930s. Popenoe's (1936, 1943) work was largely social psychological, investigating motivation leading to childless marriages, while Kucznski (1938) and Kiser (1939) explored demographic data in an attempt to study the incidence of childlessness. Popenoe's report on reasons for voluntary childlessness reflects a less-than-positive orientation toward those who opted for this lifestyle. In analyzing "reasons for voluntary refusal to bear children," Popenoe (1936) concludes that "most of the cases are purely neurotic." In a later report, Popenoe (1943) includes the following among motivations to remain childless: a general dislike of children, unhappy marriages which would be made even more unhappy by the addition of a third dependent member, economic pressures, and fear of pregnancy on the part of wives who "feared the experience would spoil their looks or figures."

During the 1940s, 1950s, and the 1960s, little interest was shown in the phenomenon of childlessness. While some attempt was made by demographers to ascertain the extent of childlessness, social psychological studies were completely lacking. With the exception of Popenoe's work, little data have appeared on why couples would decide not to bear children or on the implications of such a decision.

Veevers' (1972, 1973, 1974a, 1974b) exploratory study of childless married women in Canada contributes valuable insights on this long-neglected topic. Her study utilized in-depth interviews with 52 voluntarily childless wives who had been married at least five years. Respondents for this study were primarily middle-class, white, working women living in urban areas. Veevers' study was exploratory in nature; volunteers were solicited by newspaper articles which appeared in three separate newspapers in Toronto and London, Ontario, Canada. The criteria used to select respondents from the 86 individuals who replied to the solicitations were essentially three-fold:

(1) A statement indicating that the woman was childless by choice; there were no known biological disabilities.

(2) An affirmation concerning the woman's being married for at least five years, or was of post-menopausal age, or reported that either she or her spouse had been sterilized for contraceptive purposes;

(3) A determination that there was no evidence indicating that the woman had been a mother, either naturally or socially [Veevers, 1972].

The interviews took about four hours to complete and included information concerning the life history of the individual, including the woman's marriage and husband; and the respondent's attitudes toward the maternal role. From analysis of the data from these in-depth interviews, certain social characteristics appeared:

The average age of the sample is 29, with a range from 23 to 71 years. All are Caucasian and living in urban areas, most are middle class, and many are upwardly mobile. Although educational experiences range from grade school to the post doctoral level, most have at least some university experience. With the exception of one housewife, all are either employed full-time or attending universities. Most individuals are either atheists or agnostics from Protestant backgrounds and of the minority who do express some religious preference, almost all are inactive. Most individuals come from stable homes where the mother has been a full-time housewife since her first child was born. The incidence of first-born and only children is much higher than would ordinarily be expected [Veevers, 1973].

Definite statements concerning the voluntarily childless cannot be made from this study; however, certain tentative statements can be offered. First, the road to the decision to remain childless begins before *and* after marriage. Some respondents indicated that the childless decision was "written into their marriage 'contract'" (Veevers, 1973). For other respondents the decision came about slowly: as the couple became older, the husband and wife realized that postponement of bearing children had turned into a decision never to have children. Although the individuals experienced varying amounts of social pressure, Veevers contends that the wives had little difficulty in coping with the pressure. Adoption was cited as one mechanism that helped the wives defend against social sanctions.

In another paper which described the "moral careers" of voluntarily childless wives, Veevers (1974b) discusses the voluntarily childless as a deviant category. According to Veevers, there are a variety of social mechanisms which lead people in the direction of reproduction; those couples who choose not to be led are seen in an unfavorable light by the rest of society. Some couples Veevers studied did not express any concern about the social pressure—a fact that is rather surprising given the emphasis the society places on parenthood (Veevers, 1974b). Although the wives in Veevers' study indicated awareness of social pressure and the prevailing societal norms, they expressed indifference rather than any concern. Social pressure was exerted by "parents, in-laws, siblings, work associates, friends and doctors—from almost everyone except their husbands" (Veevers, 1974b). Social pressure may make these respondents uncomfortable, but it rarely distresses them. They are quite aware that people may strongly disagree with their decision and their views on parenthood. They are also acutely aware of "direct and indirect social sanctions apparently intended to punish them for their immoral attitudes and/or to indice them to conform to the dominant fertility norms" (Veevers, 1974b). It would appear that these wives would be somewhat bothered, yet they claim to remain relatively unperturbed. It is apparent that, with the support of their spouses, respondents are well equipped to construct a comfortable "world view justifying the variant preference for a childfree existence. The essence of this alternative construction of reality is the discrediting of one's discreditors" (Veevers, 1974b). These respondents were able to reconstruct the world's view about them in such a way to discount and question many beliefs which are regarded as unquestionable by the rest of society.

There are, according to Veevers, several basic strategies the voluntarily childless employ to defend and maintain an alternate social reality: selective perception, structuring of social situations, differential association, and societal ambivalence.

Selective perception allows the couple to concentrate on the disadvantages of having children and the advantages of remaining childfree, while remaining impervious to the compensatory aspects of parenthood.

The structuring of social situations associated with trial parenthood is such that, intentionally or not, experiences with borrowed children are unlikely to be very rewarding.

Differential association with persons who either are childless or who would like to be, reinforces the commitment to the belief system, and minimizes the danger of conversion to competing ideologies.

The fact of societal ambivalence towards parenthood allows the childless to reinterpret disapproval as envy (Veevers, 1974b). These strategies, then, help the couple to comfortably survive in social situation where their deviant worldview would otherwise cause them difficulties.

In a further development of her original study, Veevers explored the lifestyle of voluntarily childless couples. The voluntarily childless, unlike couples who become parents, do not expend their resources on the needs and special activities associated with children. Instead, Veevers describes the lifestyle of these couples in terms of *reactive* factors and *attrahent* factors, the former referring to the reactions of the couples that revolve around the disadvantages of having children, and the latter concerning the advantages of a life that is primarily centered on adult activities and interests. That is, reactive factors involve reactions to negative aspects of childlessness while attrahent factors refer to positive-type reactions. Veevers suggests that reactive factors may be such matters as observing unhappy parental marriages, atypical experiences with siblings, or lack of strategies for dealing with voluntary childlessness. Attrahent factors may include such things as extremely satisfactory marital relationships, the desire for demanding careers, or the quest for novel experiences (Veevers, 1974a). Children, it would appear, are viewed by childless couples as interfering with their lifestyle.

Mobility—the freedom to change jobs, move around the country, and so on—was considered by Veevers' respondents as an important aspect of their lifestyle. The relative affluence of couples who chose not to have children reinforces the freedom to change jobs, go to school, or otherwise change a major portion of their responsibilities. Too, the very fact that a woman is without children allows the wife the option to pursue a wide variety of alternatives, such as school, job, or virtually any other endeavor that seems to be of interest. In this way, wives are able to avoid a routine that would certainly be theirs if they were to have children. Respondents indicated they valued new experiences and they were able to pursue them only because they didn't have the responsibilities of children (Veevers, 1974a). This emphasis on new experiences would also to be an emphasis on spontaneity. The large amount of leisure time that the voluntarily childless have can be exploited to include a wide range of activities and behavioral options not open to those who bear the responsibility of childrearing.

While Veevers' findings have filled a gap in family literature, its exploratory nature leaves room for other similar studies. One major shortcoming of her research was that it included only wives. The study reported here will treat the childless couple as a couple, soliciting responses from both husbands and wives. It is the position of the authors that the decision to have or not to have children is usually made by the couple, not simply by the wife. In order to investigate such a decision, both husbands and wives must be studied. (For a discussion of the joint construction of marital reality, see Poloma and Garland, 1972.)

The present study of voluntarily childfree couples in a metropolitan area of the midwest is intended as a supplement to Veevers' exploratory research in Canada. This exploratory effort will have as its main focus the examination of the decision and commitment made by couples who remain voluntarily childless.

METHODOLOGY

The sample of 30 voluntarily childless couples was selected on a convenience basis, with eight of the initial interviews being the result of an article in the local newspaper requesting subjects for the study. These original eight interviewees referred seven additional couples, five of whom participated in the study. Another ten names were provided by friends and acquaintances of the researchers, and they in turn referred another seven couples. Although there are friendship networks in the sample, they are very limited ones. The majority of the respondents did not have close friends who were also voluntarily childless, and their acquaintances tended to include couples both with and without children.

Data were collected through a focused interview conducted by both authors. Each interview was conducted with the husband and wife separately but simultaneously, usually in the respondents' homes. Each interview lasted approximately one to one and a half hours, and all interviews were tape recorded and transcribed. Being exploratory in nature, the interview included information on the respondents' backgrounds, courtship, marriage, perceived costs and benefits of the childfree state, and career plans. Most of the questions were open-ended, thus allowing the respondent to answer in her/his own words.

Three points should be emphasized regarding the methodology of the study.

(1) Both husbands and wives were interviewed—simultaneously but separately.

(2) Collecting data from both spouses permitted the husband and wife to be treated as a single case; every attempt is made in analysis to use the couple as the unit of analysis where appropriate.

(3) The construction of reality for the couple is processual rather than static. Many of the decisions reported in this paper may be final ones. The life of a couple—or a family—is in continual process and subject to change. Attempts are made to deal with the data within the flux of change.

SOCIOECONOMIC CORRELATES OF VOLUNTARY CHILDLESSNESS

Both Veevers' exploratory research and the present study suffer from use of nonrandom sampling techniques selected because of an inability to define the population. Coupled with this problem which affects representativeness is the use of a relatively small size in both studies. What this means is that any attempt to identify the socioeconomic correlates of voluntary childlessness must be tentative. Some of the correlates coincide with those observed by Veevers, thus lending support to her observations. Others, as we shall see, are more subject to question. The appendix offers a detailed chart of the backgrounds of the respondents in the present study. Before further presentation of findings, we would like to compare these respondents with Veevers' in an attempt to identify possible structural variables that may correlate with voluntary childlessness.

COMPARISON OF WIVES' BACKGROUND CHARACTERISTICS

When the data gathered in this effort is compared with the results of Veevers' (1972) exploratory study, certain similarities are apparent. However, any comparison with Veevers' data must be done with wives rather than with couples since Veevers' work does not extend to husbands. While the N of this sample of wives is smaller than that of Veevers' (N=30 wives as compared with N=52 wives), the wives compare similarly on several variables. The all-Caucasian samples are both relatively young. The mean age of the wives in this study is 26.4 which is only slightly younger than Veevers' sample which reports a mean age of 27. The relative youth of both samples is noteworthy, given the fact that these wives are largely under 30 years of age and in the middle of their childbearing years, they have chosen not to have children. Both samples consist of well-educated women. Veevers (1972: 357) states, "Although educational experience ranges from grade school to the post-doctoral level, most have at least some university experience." The educational attainment of the wives in this study ranges from high school graduate to doctoral candidates. Only three wives have had no university experience and two of these three wives have definite plans to continue their education on the university level. Thus, 20 wives (66 percent) have a university degree, with 10 of the 20 having graduate experience or a graduate degree. Of the remaining seven wives, all were either in the midst of obtaining university degrees or had two years of college experience.

Like Veevers' sample, all of the respondents are now living in urban areas with a majority having a Protestant background (53 percent). Unlike Veevers' respondents, however, the majority of women in this sample expressed some religious preference even though only seven defined themselves as "religious." Of these seven, only one wife attended religious services more than twice a year for important religious functions, such as Christmas or weddings. The one exception, a Roman Catholic, made it clear that she attended religious services only to accompany her husband and not because she felt she was obligated to attend because of her own religious inclination.

Again, like Veevers' respondents, these wives had a higher incidence of being the first-born or the only child (N=19; first-born, N=16; only-child wives, N=3) than might be expected. Of the 16 who were the first-born, all but one wife was actively involved with caring for her siblings and, in a sense, had already experienced the motherhood role. As a result, there is little about this role of which these wives are ignorant. While they expressed confidence concerning their ability to be a "good" parent, the desire to recreate their teen-aged role is definitely lacking. Veevers (1973a: 189) argues that "motherhood for them (the first born) means sacrifice and martyrdom, and although they may feel affection, respect and sympathy for their own mother, they do not identify with her and have little desire to be like her." One woman in this sample described her experiences with her younger sisters after her mother died as follows:

> A large part of the way I feel about kids is because of my three real sisters after my mother died. I think to be 10 or 11 and to have to take care of children every day, and to go to school, come home, make dinner, do laundry and stuff—I remember thinking I'm never going to be tied down and shut in like this again [couple #24, wife].

While this respondent assumed more of the child-care responsibilities than did the other respondents, her response reflects and illustrates many of the sentiments other first-born wives expressed.

Only-children, on the other hand, express different views about their lack of siblings and their feelings about children and parenthood. As one woman commented:

> I didn't have younger brothers and sisters I had to care for—that probably has a lot to do with my attitude (toward the mother-hood role) [couple #23, wife].

The only-child wife comes from a family where she was not involved with child-care responsibilities unless she babysat or was actively involved with neighbors and/or relatives with young children. However, the three wives who are only-children in this sample were not actively involved with baby-sitting or any other activity which would expose them to prolonged obser-vations of child-care. That is, these wives come from a family background where they have not observed or experienced first hand the child-care roles adults assume with anyone but themselves. While the only-children are familiar with adults assuming parenthood roles with themselves, they do not have the opportunity to observe such roles when they are directed to others. What this tends to suggest is some support for Veevers' (1973: 184) contention:

> Voluntary childlessness may be associated with atypical experi-ences with siblings. Both the girl who has no siblings and no ex-perience with child-care and the girl who has very many siblings and very extensive experience with child-care may be more pre-disposed to challenge the motherhood mystique.

Veevers (1972) further describes her respondents as "middle-class," evidently on the basis of their lifestyle and educational attainment (al-though this is not clear in any of her published work to date). This tends to suggest that social class was determined largely on the basis of impres-sionistic observations and wives' educational attainment alone rather than by the use of any standard determinant of social position. While this in part may be due to the fact that Veevers did not directly obtain data from any of the husbands of the wives she interviewed, her basic impressions did not completely explain the social class of the couples in this study. That is, as a result of the lack of an objective means of measuring social class, Veevers' contention that her sample was middle-class cannot be general-ized to other research efforts that deal with the voluntarily childless. As a means of providing support for (or refuting of) Veevers' argument, it was decided that an objective measure of social class was desirable. Hollingshead's Two Factor Index of Social Class (1957) was utilized for computing the social class of the couples in this study. The majority of the couples are clustered in Classes I and II. The Two Factor Index of Social Position clearly shows that this sample of couples is largely middle-class based on the factors of occupation and education. Classes I and II are made up of the heads of households who have at least a standard college degree and who are employed in occupations that were determined by Hollingshead's research to belong to a particular rank. While the occupational scale developed by Hollingshead is a modification of Alba Edwards' index of the occupation classification into S.E.S. groupings, it is based upon the assumption that "occupations have different values attached to them by the members of our society. The hierarchy ranges from the low evaluation of unskilled physical labor toward the more prestigeous use of skill, through the creative talents, ideas, and the management of men" (Hollingshead and Redlich, 1958: 391). On the basis of this index, social position was computed. The data would seem to provide some support for Veevers' (1972) impressions of social class for her 52 wife-only sample. However, that 10 couples (33 percent) fall into Classes II and IV indicates that, based upon the use of the Two Factor Index, not every couple reporting a decision to remain childless can be found in the first two classes. While it is clear that the majority of the sample can be found there, it is not completely accurate to describe the sample as "totally middle-class." Moreover, couples who occupt the lowest socioeconomic status were not successfully tapped in either of the studies. This suggests two possibilities: first, the phenomenon of voluntary childlessness may indeed be a phenomenon of the middle and upper middle-classes. Support for such an expectation may be based upon mass media exposure to the consequences of overpopulation, the high level of educational attainment of both husband and wife, the consequences of the woman's liberation movement, the level of affluence of these couples, or the consequences of rapid consumption of our natural resources by overpopulation. Second, the lack of couples occupying the lower socioeconomic categories could be attributed to the method of acquiring a sample which was employed by both research efforts. Both studies obtained their samples through local newspapers and/or the use of snowballing to obtain a wider sample.

LIFESTYLE OF THE VOLUNTARILY CHILDLESS

Veevers (1974a) asserts that most adults structure much of their adult lives in such a way as to take into account the demands of child-care. The voluntarily childless are not faced with such responsibilities and their lifestyle reflects this adult-centered lifestyle. The respondents in this study valued their leisure time, spending it reading, watching and engaging in sports, visiting and entertaining, traveling, dining out, and attending movies, plays, and concerts. Almost without exception the respondents indicated that the activities they engaged in, while they could be enjoyed alone, were redefined in terms of what the couple do together. That is, these couples indicated that they would prefer to spend their leisure hours with each other, rather than alone or with others.

The amount of time these couples spend with each other by mutual choice and their activities are structured or restructured so that spouses can be with each other. Veevers (1974a) suggests that voluntarily childless couples, in the process of developing a new social reality which involves the gradual exclusion of other people, carry this process to its logical extreme. She contends that in such a process of constructing a new social reality, the couple begins to view each other as a "reference group of one." The inclusion of children would make such a reference group impossible. Shifting from such a relationship to one in which children would be a part is not viewed as desirable; the presence of a third member would forever disrupt the contentment experienced in the intense dyadic relationship of the voluntarily childless. Veevers (1974a) argues that "a dominant component is commitment to the ideal that a married couple should be a self-sufficient unit, who look to each other for the satisfaction of most (and perhaps all) of their social and psychological needs." This is certainly evidenced by the couples in this sample who indicate that their spouses fulfill most, if not all, of their social needs. Voluntarily childless couples seem to consider that a third member, a child, would endanger the satisfaction attained in the marital dyad. This attitude was reflected time and again in comments made by both husbands and wives:

> I saw what happened to my friends' minds and marriages after they had kids [couple #30, wife].

> Children would be a detriment to the kind of marital relationship I want [couple #22, husband].

> I like the aspect of having one person who is closer to you emotionally than any other person—a person with whom you can very intimately interact, both mentally and physically [couple #23, husband].

The absence of children was viewed as something positive to the marital relationship; the presence of children was considered to be detrimental to an intimate husband-wife relationship. Couples were concerned about the strain that a child would put on their now satisfactory marriage:

> Having a child would put a strain on our relationship because we would not be as accessible to each other; we couldn't be together alone as often. We value that. Having a child would mean that we would be really tied down [couple #24, husband].

> I would be jealous of the time my husband and I would not have alone together because I married for companionship. There would be so many things we couldn't do that I think my whole outlook on marriage would have to change quite a bit in order to make room for a child. A whole lot of things in our relationship would have to change, and I'm happy with our relationship the way it is now. I am not anxious to change it for a child [couple #23, wife.].

These and other similar comments would indicate that the couples perceive that they would not enjoy their relationships, and each other, as much if they were to have a child. Veevers' (1974a) work is supportive of this contention. It seems as if the voluntarily childless want nothing to interfere with their marital relationships, and parenthood is seen as a potential threat to their satisfactory dyadic union. As long as the childfree lifestyle is rewarding, there appear to be serious hesitations about introducing any change in the marriage.

The voluntarily childless couples in this sample did not tend to join organizations nor do they tend to know more than one other couple who is also voluntarily childfree. Wives tend to join more organizations than their husbands ($\overline{X}=1.5$, husbands and $\overline{X}=2.3$, wives) although neither spouse tends to be active in those organizations. This provides further evidence to support the contention that people who elect to be childless appear to be content with the company and companionship provided by their spouses. As one wife states, "We simply aren't joiners." Aside from the fact that they are not joiners, the voluntarily childless do not appear to be acquainted with others who do not have children. Having children or not having children is not viewed as a criterion for another couple's friendship; all that is required is an acceptance of the childless couple's chosen lifestyle. Most respondents had never heard of the National Organization for Non-parents (NON), and the vast majority saw no need for such an organization. Their response regarding NON fits in with their general reluctance to become involved in organized efforts and their acceptance of friendship offered by couples with children.

INCOME AND ITS RELATION TO LIFESTYLES

Without the responsibility of financially supporting children, the couples in our sample naturally had more of their income to earmark for leisure and luxuries than do couples with similar incomes who are parents. The joint incomes of the respondents ($\bar{X}=\$16,400$) seem to be high enough for the couple to support a solidly middle-class lifestyle. The advantages of a joint income were mentioned time and again by the couples, and this monetary advantage seemed to play an important role in remaining child-less. Further, since only two wives were unemployed at the time of the interview, the employment or career of the wife appeared to be closely tied with the jointness of reported income. That is, the couples were very much aware of the fact that their incomes and expenditures would be greatly affected by the arrival of a child, and that this would necessitate a drastic change in lifestyle.

The vast majority of the couples rented apartments rather than pur-chasing single-unit dwellings. Most liked the freedom they found in being apartment dwellers. Even though 23 couples (77 percent) rent apartments, these residences are well-furnished with articles, such as expensive stereos and fine furniture, which could not have been afforded on one salary alone. Couples were very much aware of what a decrease in income would mean if children entered their lives; the monetary advantages in supporting two people as opposed to three or four seemingly is viewed as a benefit not to be overlooked or discounted.

WIVES' CAREER CONSIDERATIONS

All of the wives who were working indicated that they intended to continue in their chosen careers. When asked why they were working, wives invariably responded that they "would be bored staying home." Perhaps because of the high educational attainment of these wives, they appear to be extremely attached to the idea of working in a career that brings satisfaction and a reasonable income. Commitment to a job or ca-reer is highly valued by the wives, and the husbands in this sample were also cognizant of the importance of their wives' work. Indeed many hus-bands commented that the very idea that their spouses like to work was one of the precipitating factors attracting them. While it was not the pur-pose of the research to determine whether or not the wives in the sample were "career" as opposed to "job" oriented, it remains clear that the wives define themselves as occupationally oriented, as do their husbands.

Most wives felt that they would continue working even if (due to accident or change of mind) they had a child. Only 20 percent asserted that they would cease working if they had a child. Most felt that having a child would make little difference in their basic orientation toward their employment situations. It is important to point out, however, that most of the women were employed in jobs with regular hours in work that did not require traveling. They did recognize that in the event they had a child, the brunt of child-care and child-rearing would be assumed by the wives. Given the fact that the women liked being employed outside the home and both husbands and wives were satisfied with their marital situation, having children was viewed as an unnecessary complication and burden.

A TYPOLOGY OF COMMITMENT: A REFLECTION OF THE DECISION-MAKING PROCESS

One of the clearest issues to emerge from the data was the fact that not all 30 couples were equally committed to remaining childless. Even though the interviewers stressed to each potential respondent couple that the purpose of the research was to study the *permanently* and *voluntarily* childless, it became apparent during the course of the interviews that the degree of resolve varied among the respondents. Based upon the responses to four critical questions, a four-fold typology emerged which encompassed the degree of commitment reflected by each couple These four categories are

(1) the irrevocably committed,
(2) the strongly committed,
(3) the reasonably committed, and
(4) the committed with reservations.

Placement within any one category was based upon the score attained by the couple's responses to the following items:

Criteria	Weight	Highest Possible Score Per Couple
Contraceptive use:		
Effective users	5	5
Somewhat effective users	3	
No contraceptive use	0	

Abortion (in the event of an unwanted pregnancy):		
Definitely yes (wife only response)	4	4
Maybe (wife)	2	
Definitely no (wife)	0	
Sterilization:		
Yes, in the future	2	4
Maybe, thoutht about it	1	
No, never	0	
Possibility of children in the future:		
No	2	4
Possibly, not sure	1	
Yes	0	
		17

For the abortion issue, the wife's response was the one considered since husbands tended to suggest that any decision concerning abortion would ultimately be left up to their wives; it would be the wives who would have to undergo the actual abortion.

Scores were computed based upon husband/wife responses to the above, with the exception of the abortion issue. The highest score a couple could obtain is 17. Couples who have one or both spouses sterilized were immediately placed in the first category, the Irrevocably Committed, and were assigned a weight of 21. The couples placed themselves accordingly:

Type	Couple I.D. Numbers	Weight
Category I: Irrevocably Committed	#7, #13, #16, #19, #22	21
Category II: Strongly Committed	#2, #4, #11, #14, #15, #21, #24, #29	14 - 17
Category III: Reasonably Committed	#1, #3, #5, #6, #8, #9, #10, #12, #17, #18, #23, #30	10 – 13
Category IV: Committed with Reservations	#20, #25, #26, #27, #28	7 – 9

We want to emphasize the fact that all of these couples had reported themselves to be permanently and voluntarily childfree during the initial telephone interview. The couples in categories III and IV might be just as likely as couples in categories I and II to inform their friends and families that they have chosen to remain childless—they may even themselves believe that they have permanently chosen such a status. The data gathered during the course of the interviews, however, suggest otherwise. There is no question that the degree of commitment of the couples in categories III and IV is not as great as those in the first two categories. It is possible that some of the couples will become parents, either through an accidental pregnancy that they chose not to have aborted or through a reevaluation of their childfree state of life. We would like to illustrate each of the types of commitment with cases from our sample.

Category I: The Irrevocably Committed

In these five couples, one or both partners in the marriage had been sterilized to avoid unwanted pregnancy. Three of these couples were in their mid to late 20s, with the other two couples being over 35 years of age. One couple considered themselves to be "very religious," but neither the husband nor the wife had attended religious services within the past year. The other four couples identified themselves as nonreligious with no church membership or preference. The income level for all five couples was between $16,000 and $20,000. All except one husband and one wife (not married to each other) held at least a bachelor's degree, with the majority holding graduate degrees. The sole criterion for placing couples into Category I was either male or female sterilization. In four cases the wife had had a tubal ligation; two husbands had vacectomies. One of our cases, whom we will call the Hortons, provide a profile of the irrevocably committed category and its decision-making process.

Mrs. Horton is 27 years old and is employed as a secretary; her husband is 29 and works in the business profession. They have been married for five years and it is a first marriage for both. Like the overwhelming majority of our respondents, they did not discuss remaining childless before marriage. Mr. Horton commented,

> Before we were married, we had talked about having four children. When we were first married, we were usually pretty busy during the day. The only time we talked to each other was when we were lying in bed before we would fall asleep. We would lie in bed some nights trying to think up names for four kids.

Mrs. Horton reported that they had made their decision not to have children about a year after they married; Mr. Horton said it was within two years after marriage. While the actual decision-making process is lost in their family history, Mr. Horton says he remembers the night he first brought up the possibility of remaining permanently childless.

> I guess we were married, probably about two years or so as I recall, when one night I said to Mary, "How would you feel about having no children?" She said, "I've been thinking about that myself." We talked about it more, and as time went on, that became our decision—we were not going to have any children. It was a mutual thing, with each of us reaching our own decision.

Mr. Horton heard that some men were having medical difficulties after vasectomies and he was reluctant to have one. He and Mrs. Horton agreed that female sterilization was now safer than it had been and is now also relatively easy. Mrs. Horton had a tubal ligation after four years of marriage at the age of 26.

There is evidence from the couple's report that the final decision not to have children was made over time and was not without guilt. The feelings of guilt appear now to be well under control. Mr. Horton observed:

> We thought about adopting a child, but we probably will not. I think there was some guilt carry-over when we decided not to have children. We thought, "That's not natural. Well, if we are not going to have children of our own, there are a lot of unloved and unwanted kids who could use a home." I think we have grown away from adopting. I want to help kids—maybe as a volunteer Big Brother—but I don't want to have any.

Our sample is too small to observe any common or divergent background patterns among the couples. Even the strength of the wife's career commitment, which judging from other respondents undoubtedly has some bearing on childlessness, is not a constant for couples in this category. Mrs. Horton is employed outside the home (one other wife is not), but Mrs. Horton clearly sees her job as "secondary to my husband's." What is common to the couples is an irrevocable decision not to have children. At this stage in time it is difficult, if not impossible, to determine which member of the couple was more instrumental in the decision-making process or whether it was truly a mutual, simultaneous decision as they tend to report. Only one of the five couples, a couple who married after age 30, had decided to remain childless prior to their marriage. For the remaining couples it was a gradual decision reached after marriage.

Category II: The Strongly Committed

The eight couples were classified on the bases of the following four criteria:

(1) they were all "effective users" of contraception (all eight women were taking "the pill");

(2) both the husband's and the wife's discussion of sterilization revealed no fears about the irrevocability of the surgicial procedure;

(3) in the case of contraceptive failure, both husband and wife expressed the belief that the wife would have an abortion rather than bear the child; and

(4) there were no signs in the interview that either the husband or the wife was ambivalent about their reported decision.

The Jameses provide an illustration of a strongly committed couple. Mr. and Mrs. James have been married for three years and have a combined income of $26,000. Mrs. James is 25; her husband is 26. They have no religious preference, although two other couples in this category are practicing Protestants. The Jameses have discussed sterilization only in passing. Mrs. James feels that she will have done her part in keeping them childfree by taking the pill, which she plans to do for another six or seven years. After 10 years of marriage, Mrs. James said she would expect her husband to obtain a vasectomy. Both she and Mr. James appear unaware that other childless couples their age have succeeded in obtaining sterilizations; neither is aware of the simplification of the tubal ligation technique. Mr. James claims he has not seriously considered sterilization because *he* has not ruled out the possibility of having children. He would consider having a vasectomy only if his wife could no longer take the pill. As a couple the Jameses are resolved not to have children, but Mr. James would not be opposed to having children if this relationship ended. He commented:

> I am not going to rule out anything. Let's say Sally were to die. If I met a woman with children who was widowed or divorced, that would not preclude me from marrying her. Nor would a woman's feeling that she wanted a family. If that was definitely what she wanted, that would be all right with me.

In analyzing the Jameses situation we find a young woman who is very career-oriented with no desire for children. Unlike most of our respondents, Mrs. James was cognizant of her feelings before marriage since she had been a mother-substitute for her younger siblings. Although it was not easy for her, she made it clear to her husband before they were married that she did not want children. Mrs. James recalled:

> I knew before I got married that I didn't want children and I told Hal that. It wasn't that he wanted children—he wasn't sure. I don't think that he believed me at first when I said I was positive that I did not want children. We discussed it again and I told him not to count on me changing my mind. I didn't want to get married under false pretenses.

Mr. James was under no illusions and accepts childlessness as a condition of their apparently highly satisfactory interpersonal relationship. He sees that if they did have a child, the cost would be much higher for his wife than for him:

> I can't imagine Sally being a mother and housewife—not even for a couple of years. That interruption in her career would not be good for her, and I don't think I would like it either. If we did decide to have children, it would be because Sally wanted to. I can see where she would bear more of the burden of having children than I would.

In all eight of these cases it was the wife who was strongly committed to not having children, and the husband was supportive of this decision for that particular relationship. No husband interviewed felt lacking due to the absence of paternity and all were able to stress the many advantages of a childfree marriage. In another relationship, these men may have become fathers. It is highly unlikely, however, that any of these *couples* will have a child in the future.

Category III: The Reasonably Committed

The reasonably committed couples differed from those in the first two categories in that they either expressed some minor doubts about the permanency of their decision or expressed concern about what course of action they would follow in the event of contraceptive failure. All 12 couples were effective users of contraceptives (the pill, regular use of the diaphragm, or condom and foam) and probably (although they were not certain) would have an abortion if an unwanted pregnancy would occur. The mean age of these couples was 25.4, nearly a year younger than the 26.3 years for the strongly committed. With the exception of one couple, all respondents have attended college; eight have bachelor's degrees, 10 have masters degrees or have attended graduate school. Of the 24 respondents, 13 identified themselves as being either Protestant or Roman Catholic, although none of them are regular attenders of church services.

These couples appear to be still in the process of working through the decision to remain permanently childfree within the context of their marriages, but they are definitely leaning toward a permanent commitment. They are simply not as certain of what the future may bring (particularly in the event of a contraceptive failure) as the couples in Categories I and II. Mr. and Mrs. Banning provide an illustration of reasonable commitment.

Mr. and Mrs. Banning have both done some graduate work. Mrs. Banning is 26 years of age and employed as a social worker; Mr. Banning is 28 and works for a small business firm. Their combined income is over $25,000. In common with most of the wives in this category, Mrs. Banning expressed a stronger desire not to have children than did her husband. She noted:

> I am more committed to not having children than Marty is. Actually, we're both rather selfish and like our lives the way they are. I know I am not willing to give up my job or career or whatever you want to call it to devote myself to being a full-time mother, and I don't know that I could handle both. I like my freedom; I like to be able to pick up and go and do pretty much what I want to do and when I want to do it. I'm not sure I am willing to make the sacrifices and face the responsibilities of parenthood.

Mrs. Banning also informed the interviewer several times during the interview that she does not particularly enjoy contact with children, although her husband claims that he does. Yet both Mr. and Mrs. Banning are reluctant to close the door completely on the possibility of having children.

Mrs. Banning is on the pill, so contraceptive failure is not likely. If an unwanted pregnancy were to occur, however, Mrs. Banning is not sure whether she would be able to go through with an abortion. She attributes this to her Roman Catholic background and convent school education, although she does not rule out *consideration* of an abortion as an alternative to parenthood and feels that she would likely go through with it as a "lesser of two evils." Mr. and Mrs. Banning have both talked about sterilization, but neither is particularly well informed about the topic. Mr. Banning said that "I want to wait another four years to be absolutely certain. If we can find a doctor, I will have a vasecetomy." Mrs. Banning concurs that in four years (when they are both past 30 years of age) some definite decision will have to be made about sterilization, although she thinks her husband is afraid of facing surgery. Most likely the Bannings will continue to drift in their childfree state of life; if pregnancy were to occur, it would be difficult at this point to accurately predict what they would do.

As couples who are effective users of contraceptives, who are not morally opposed to abortion and who enjoy the freedom of childlessness, it is unlikely that couples in Category III will bear children. But their plans and visions are not as strongly focused as are the strongly committed.

Category IV: Committed with Reservations

Five couples were categorized as being committed with reservations. All were effective users of contraception, but were less enthusiastic about sterilization or abortion. Possibly due to their realization that pregnancy was a possibility, they expressed some doubt about the permanency of their decision. The mean age for the husbands and wives in this category is 28.6 years as compared with 25.4 years for the reasonably committed, demonstrating that age alone is not a determining factor in the strength of commitment for those in our sample. Most were college graduates, with one husband holding a doctorate. Six of the 10 respondents identified themselves as either Roman Catholic or Protestant, although like most of the rest of the sample, none of them attended religious services regularly. The mean family income was $20,000.

The issue of abortion separated these couples from the reasonably committed. These wives were disposed against abortion and may have stated flatly that they would not even consider an abortion in the event of an unwanted pregnancy. It is difficult to know whether, if faced with a loss of income, freedom, and career, these wives would change their minds and opt for an abortion, but their attitude now is at best one of ambivalence. This ambivalence is also reflected in both the husbands' and wives' uncertainty as to whether they will remain permanently childless. (All respondents, including these five couples, volunteered for the interviews and professed to be permanently childless.) Mr. and Mrs. Carter provide an illustration of the uncertainty and ambivalence facing these five couples.

Mr. and Mrs. Carter both have college degrees; Mr. Carter also has attended graduate school. Both have taught in high schools and have been exposed to children only on that level. Mrs. Carter is ambivalent about the abortion issue:

> I have zero opposition to abortion in general, but if it were *me*, I don't know—I just don't know. If the situation were to occur now, I would be obliged to have the child for several reasons.

First of all, if I had a child, I would be a good parent. I could afford to have a child. My child, if I were to have one now, would not be starving for anything—food, clothing, affection, anything. If circumstances were different, it would make a big difference. The reason I would hesitate is because it would be 100 percent selfish. Once it happened, I probably would keep it.

Apparently, if there is no contraceptive failure, Mrs. Carter will remain childless. She fears the "terribly frightening responsibility of children." She also feels the pressure of her mother's wanting her to give her a grandchild. Mr. Carter says "it doesn't make any difference" whether they have children or not. He will support his wife in either the decision to have or not to have children.

Mrs. Carter says she does not like children, although her husband claims that he does. While she enjoys her work as an educational assistant, Mrs. Carter does not think of it in terms of a career. She claims she is not anxious to "move up the ladder," seeing her husband as more career-oriented than she. She also claims that she "would be a fool to say I would *never* have children." Mrs. Carter does not want to irrevocably commit herself to a childfree life—"There is always the possibility that I will reconsider my decision not to have children." She and her husband have not discussed sterilization as a means of avoiding the pregnancy they both claim they do not want. (It is of interest to note that two other couples in our sample know the Carters and both believed them to be very strongly committed to nonparenthood.)

Couples in the other categories were either convinced they would terminate an unwanted pregnancy or leaned strongly toward the possibility of so doing. Couples in Category IV claimed, for the most part, that at this point in time they would go through with an unwanted pregnancy and adjust to parenthood. This fact is coupled with an uncertainty as to whether they might change their minds and *plan* for a family. In the other three categories there was little, if any, serious discussion of such a drastic mind change.

SOCIETAL PRESSURE AND THE TYPOLOGY OF COMMITMENT

It is apparent from the foregoing disucssion that not all couples are equally committed to remaining childless. Given the cultural stress on the importance of children for fulfillment, we questioned whether perceived outside pressure from family and friends might be related to the strength of commitment. We hypothesized that the stronger the commitment, the less the perceived pressure; the weaker the commitment, the more the pressure to have children would be perceived by the couple. We also hypothesized that husbands were less likely to perceive pressure to have children than were their wives. Overall, both hypotheses appeared to receive limited support; but due to the small sample size, it is difficult to do any more than to suggest a direction of relationship.

As was expected, the irrevocably committed and the strongly committed couples perceived little or no pressure from family and friends to have children. Negative reactions were most likely to come from acquaintances who were not perceived by the couples to be part of their reference group. There was little difference between husbands' and wives' perceptions of such pressure.

The reasonably committed were most likely to be aware of societal pressures to have children, and the wives were much more likely than husbands to report incidents of such pressure. Most of the reported pressure came from the couples' parents, although in most cases it tended to be very subtle. One husband commented:

> The biggest sadness of not having children will be the affect that it has on my mother. I don't think my father will pressure us; he seems to understand it. My in-laws seem to accept it. But my mother does bother me. I don't think she will ever come to accept it or to understand. I know she wants to be a grandmother—all of her friends are. I don't think it's worth having children just to please my mother, but it does bother me [couple #18, husband].

Many couples reported either a lack of parental understanding in their desire to remain childless or parents' insistence that the young couple will "change their minds" about their decision. As one husband observed:

> My parents are aware of our decision not to have children. They seem to accept that decision and have respect for our wishes. I am sure, however, that they do not understand our reasoning. My wife's mother is sure that we will change our minds. Her father stays out of our personal lives and does not express an opinion one way or the other [couple #19, wife].

While couples are able to select friends who are sympathetic toward their decision to remain childless, parents were a more fixed reference group. Few parents were able to express support for their children's decision; at best, parental attitude tended to be one of acceptance and respect for their children's right to parent or not to parent. At worst, pressure might be exerted in an attempt to cause a "mind change." Some couples where parental opposition to their childlessness had once been a problem asserted that living geographically apart from one or both set of parents greatly facilitated making a decision to remain childless.

The five couples who were committed with reservations did not tend to support the hypothesis regarding the degree of commitment and perception of societal pressures. Unexpectedly, they were more likely than the reasonably committed to assert that they experience little or no pressure to have children. This may be due to their attempt to portray their situation as one that is completely in their control. Some of these couples seemed intent upon presenting the image of their voluntary childlessness as a situation that might be subject to change—but it would be change that they, the couple, would initiate. In reality, an unplanned pregnancy could be the event that would precipitate parenthood for these couples, but they chose to stress the voluntariness of their either having or not having children.

Regardless of the degree of commitment, the vast majority of the couples in our sample did not perceive the social pressure that Veevers (1974: 2) argues is present. Veevers notes that many of her respondents reported that in the past, various "pressures had left them feeling uncomfortable and upset" although "very few reported that they were still distressed by them." Furthermore, the very few incidents that were reported as situations of societal pressure were perceived as ignorance on the part of the actors in the situation. In general, they tend to minimize, whenever possible, any instances of outside pressure to have children. As one young husband commented:

> Pressure can come from many sources—it doesn't have to be people. You can get pressure from the media, but I have learned to cope with that. That is still present. I am talking about things like the family plans for United Airlines. Things like this tends to play on the family being defined as having children. You see that often. You talk about a man and a wife when talking about a couple, but a man, a wife and children when talking about a family. *Does it bother you?* It doesn't bother me any more. My job has put me in a position to see that propaganda about family growth has enabled economic growth. Things are measured by households. I can see the media in terms of the growth of our economy—from a business perspective. I can see the ads are profit motivated. I don't like it; other people may not be able to cope with it [couple #13, husband].

Commitment to childlessness is not only related to perception of outside pressures to have children, but also to earnestness in discussing the decision not to parent with outsiders. Table 2 demonstrates the relationship between the response to the questioning of outsiders and the degree

TABLE 2
Couples' Response to "When Are You Going to Have Children?" and the Typology of Commitment

	Irrev.	Strongly	Reasonably	Reservations	
Tell the Truth	8 (80%)	13 (81%)	10 (42%)	0 (0%)	31
Lie	2 (20%)	3 (19%)	13 (54%)	4 (40%)	22
Don't Respond	0 (0%)	0 (0%)	1 (4%)	6 (60%)	7
	10	16	24	10	60

of commitment. When asked, "What do you tell people when they ask, 'When are you going to have children?'" over half the respondents replied that they simply told the truth. The irrevocably committed and the strongly committed felt the least pressure to avoid the question or to make up an excuse for their childlessness. Other couples are more likely to try to circumvent the question (for example, by responding with a joke) or to respond filippantly that they may have children in a few years.

In response to an identical question in a study of childlessness conducted by Hoover and Benson (1974), the respondents also indicated a willingness to admit their voluntary childlessness to outsiders. This would suggest that voluntarily childless couples, in both studies, did not experience or perceive enough societal pressure to force them to either lie or circumvent the question. Most husbands and wives felt comfortable in discussing their decision with others who were earnestly interested in their decision-making process or even with those who were simply "curious." Little difference was found in husbands' and wives' responses, although a slightly greater number of husbands would try to avoid the question, if possible.

CHILDLESSNESS VS. PARENTHOOD: COSTS AND BENEFITS OF A CHILDFREE LIFESTYLE

As in most societies, Americans are encouraged to concentrate on the advantages and rewards of having children rather than the disadvantages and costs of parenthood. Social, emotional, and financial costs are usually not examined by prospective parents. Popular authors Peck (1971), Silverman and Silverman (1971), and Radl (1973) have forcefully argued that such costs should be weighed carefully before a couple decides to have a child. The couples who participated in this research effort appear to engage in a process of weighing such costs and benefits associated with remaining childless. For the 30 couples in this sample, the benefits of remaining childless far outweigh any perceived costs; indeed, respondents were hard-pressed to articulate any costs or disadvantages for *their* remaining permanently childless.

As Veevers (1973a: 185) observes, one cannot simply ask the childless how and why they came to a decision not to have children and expect a coherent and accurate reply. Respondents who have been very articulate in responding to other items during the interview encounter are suddenly incapable of formulating an answer when asked how they came to decide against having children. There seemed to be three different paths the couples in this sample followed in arriving at the decision to remain childless. The first path involved making the decision not to parent before marriage (N=4 couples). In each case, it was the wife who reported first approaching the topic with her husband. One wife, who knew as a teenager that she didn't want children explained her situation as follows:

> I knew before I got married that I didn't want children, and I told Mike that. It wasn't that he definitely wanted children; he wasn't sure and I don't think he believed me when I said I was positive. I think he thought that I might change my mind. This bothered me after we first discussed it; I didn't want to get married under false pretenses. I told him that he could not count on my changing my mind [couple #24, wife].

For couples in this sample who decided before their marriages that children were not to be a part of their future, it seems that the wife was responsible for initiating the decision as illustrated by the comments of Wife #24. The reasons for the decision not to parent were as varied as the number of cases reporting a premarital decision. No pattern of common experiences could be observed. It seemed that all four of these wives were strongly motivated not to have children, knew their own minds in this regard, and met men who were supportive of their wishes and who did not particularly desire fatherhood.

The vast majority of couples in our sample, however, decided not to have children after they married. The second path that couples in this sample followed involved a decision being made within two to three years after marriage (N=12 couples). Typically the couple had not discussed either having children or not having them before marriage. Shortly after marrying they began to discuss the prospect of remaining childless and they describe their decision against parenthood as being a mutual one. The precise manner in which this decision had been reached is lost in the couples' respective histories; however, they are able to recount part of the process. For these couples the decision was a gradual one in which conversations might revolve around the problems of childrearing and the costs children might incur against their marital relationship.

The greatest number of couples (N=14) made their decision to remain childless after more than three years of married life. The decision in these cases was a result of a continued postponement of childbearing until some vague future point in time. As one husband expressed his and his wife's situation:

> Well, it wasn't something that decided instantly; it was a gradual process. When we first got married, I had only put in one year of

law school. I also got drafted that same year. When I first went into the air force, the pay was so low that it was economically impossible to have children. We had discussed having children before and after marriage, and we did decide that we both wanted children. But because of the economic situation, we postponed having them. We decided that it would not be feasible to have children until after I was out of the service and after I completed law school.

During this interim we gradually moved away from the desire to have children. It was not a quick decision. We first questioned the idea of having children about four years ago. Had I not gone into the service and had I not been in law school—had I been out working instead—I think it is very conceivable that within the first two years of marriage, we would have had children. The longer we postponed having children, the more time we had to think about it. I think it was sort of a fate thing. Having children was not feasible when we first married, and during the interim, we reached the decision that we did not want to have children [couple #18, husband].

The wife concurred about the basic process, but her account was briefer and her time sequence did not completely coincide with her husband's:

We made the decision in steps. I was never very excited about having children. I just sort of took it for granted that it was in the future. Then I started thinking about the possibility of not having to have children. Maybe there was that option. Then we made the decision that we definitely were not going to have children; we were going to take the option. During that period we had met a couple who had made precisely that decision, and I think they were the ones who made me see that there indeed was another option. We met this couple while T. was still in the air force, and I first started thinking about not having children about two years after we married [couple #18, wife].

Such couples initially wanted children, or at least were reconciled to the idea that all married couples had them, but postponed having children until a more convenient time. When they first married, these couples were not aware of the option of a childfree lifestyle. With continual postponements, the assumption that children would be part of the future faded in favor of childlessness. As another wife commented:

We did not get married with the idea that we were not going to have children. It has been a building kind of process as to choosing a lifestyle. We weren't really ready to make a final decision until we made the marriage work for 10 years or so. [This couple has been sterilized.] During those 10 years we had always considered that eventually we would have children; we simply kept putting it off. I think both of us felt that you got married, saved and acquired certain things, and then you had children. There just wasn't any question about it when we first married [couple #16, wife].

Thus in most cases, the decision not to have children was one that was reached over time during the marriage. In many instances it was a very gradual process—so gradual that it is difficult for respondents to do more than recount the most salient points. While the overall decision reported by both husbands and wives coincided, the specifics of how the decision not to have children was reached are not always in agreement. It appeared that in most cases the wife was the first one to consider not having children and the husband supported the cues she began to give about not wanting children at all.

The component of advantages and disadvantages to parenthood is one that we felt would be a crucial part of the decision-making process. As expected, couples did weigh the advantages of remaining childless and tended to minimize any potential disadvantages. It is to this topic that we will now turn our attention.

Perceived Advantages of Childless Marriages

Directly involved in the decision to remain childless, no matter what path was followed by the couple in this sample, was a weighing of the costs and benefits associated with the decision. All respondents readily delineated the advantages or benefits of remaining childless but could not as easily and readily delineate the disadvantages or costs. The five advantages cited most often were (in order of frequency): personal freedom, monetary advantages, better marital relationship without children, the importance of the wife's career, and helping to curb overpopulation.

Personal freedom and the monetary advantage seemed to go hand in hand. Respondent indicated that freedom, not only from the responsibility of child-rearing, but also from the point of view of what could be done with available resources, was of paramount importance. That is, freedom *from* child-rearing responsibilities as well as freedom *for* their own pursuits was equally stressed by respondents. Veevers (1973a: 192) also found a preoccupation of her respondents with freedom—"freedom to be geographically or occupationally mobile, freedom for leisure-time pursuits, and freedom to act spontaneously." This freedom was coupled with the monetary advantage of having two incomes without the expenditures of child-care. Respondents commented:

> With two incomes and no other mouths to feed, we're able to live at a lifestyle that's quite a bit higher than our contemporaries who have children. We can live the way we want without worrying about the financial aspects. We have endless communication because my wife works and we can stimulate each other, rather than if she were a housewife. We can do other things when we want—it (being childless) gives us a lot of freedom [couple #12, husband].

> I see all kinds of advantages but they're generally regarded as selfish although I don't know that's valid. Financially there's no question—people who don't have children have more money and can do all sorts of things people with children can't. You can be closer and have the opportunity to do a variety of things. You have more time, more money, you can get to know yourself better. All the things I want preclude my having children [couple #22, wife].

> There are a lot of advantages. Just the freedom we can have—the time we can spend with each other as opposed to the time we would have to devote to children. My wife and I can do a lot more things, spend a lot more time talking and doing things together than we could if we had children. There is the benefit to our relationship. There is the benefit to our lives in general because of the flexibility it allows us. I could consider changing jobs. We could move and not have to worry about tearing a kid away from school There's a greater level of freedom [couple #19, husband].

From the foregoing comments by some of the respondents who participated in this sample, it can be seen that the voluntarily childless place particular importance upon the interdependence of freedom, the financial resources to take advantage of that freedom, and the increased opportunity to experience an intense dyadic relationship which the previous advantages afford them.

Population and environmental concerns were only infrequently mentioned as a benefit of a childfree lifestyle. When they were mentioned, such concerns were viewed as being socially acceptable to others. Some couples tended to "use" this particular reason for maintaining their childless status when they interact with some friends and acquaintances on a social basis. Most of these couples were not environmental crusaders; rather they simply used a socially acceptable reason (and one that was less "selfish") for not having children.

Perceived Disadvantages of Childless Marriages

It was anticipated that the advantages assessed by a couple would outweigh any perceived disadvantages associated with remaining childless. Indeed couples were hard-pressed in many cases to respond when asked, "What disadvantages do you see in being voluntarily childless?" The factors most often cited were that they might regret the decision when they grew old and the corresponding "lonely old age," some social disadvantages (parents associating with other parents because of children's friendship), and the tax structure. But even when citing these "disadvantages," couples tend to try to refute them. As one husband commented:

> I must admit, there have been times that I thought I should have children. I can remember times of being frightened and getting old without having children to make me feel good. But recently I have been thinking that, if I have to become 80 years old and have to depend on my children for whatever they may want to give me, then my life won't be worth a whole lot. I'd rather look at life as striving and always moving toward something—even when I am 80 years old. Now I think that I will never need children. The biggest reason I have decided not to have them is that I do not have a strong desire for them. I think it would be really foolish on my part to have them as an experiment or as a safeguard against loneliness in old age [couple #28, husband].

Another wife was even stronger in her refusal to have children as some kind of safe deposit against old age:

> One of the biggest arguments people use about not having a family is "What are you going to do when you are old?" I find that a bad reason to have a family because you are using peope in that respect. You are having a family because you are going to become dependent on them when you get older. I think it would be hard to have these children grow up and be independent, if in the back of your mind you are going to be dependent upon them. I find a lot of people who say they have a good relationship with their adult children are almost exploiting them. That's no reason to have a family, and that's the only reason people have given me to have children. What then if you have a family and they leave you alone; what do you do then? I just find that to be a poor excuse to have a family. People say that by not having children you become very self-centered and very selfish. I think for people who are normally that way, having children or not having them does not make any difference. Those who are self-centered people will be self-centered parents. Maybe my reasons are not good for not wanting children, but I haven't heard any good ones for having them either [couple #19, wife].

Both husbands and wives commented again and again that a fear of being neglected in old age was not reason enough to have children. Some commented that they did not want their parents to be dependent upon them—and that their parents did not want to be a burden to their adult children. Most felt that there was no way that adult children could really prevent loneliness in old age.

Social disadvantages were less frequently mentioned and revolved around social contacts that parents have through their children which the voluntarily childless couples feel that they may miss. Closely related to this was the social status of being a parent. As one husband observed:

> There are some disadvantages to remaining childless. Not being able to partake in the teaching process of a person. That lack of experience may be a disadvantage. There are also some disadvantages for prestige purposes—marching down and putting your son on a merry-go-round—that type of thing. At that particular moment it may be a disadvantage because you don't have something to be proud of [couple #13, husband].

There is also some indication that childless couples may feel misunderstood by some relatives and friends. One young wife recounted the following incident:

> My aunt thought that we would not be excited when my cousin and his wife had a child, and that really incensed me. The fact that my husband and I don't want children doesn't mean that we can't be joyful for someone who does. My aunt's reaction really hurt my feelings. I was just thrilled when I saw my cousin's child; it's beautiful. There was a hint of "I'm glad it's you and not me" in the back of my mind, but I am really happy for him. They didn't think they could have children, so they were thrilled with the baby. And I am thrilled for them [couple #14, wife].

Undoubtedly other such incidents may have arisen for other couples, but they were not reported. It seemed as if couples stressed the advantages of their situation and tended to repress any regrets they feared or potential disadvantages. Most parents could talk about the joys of experiencing new life, the baby's first step or first word, junior's Cub Scout award, or Mary's winning a scholarship. There are advantages as well as disadvantages to parenthood. These couples, even under intense probing, chose to stress the advantages of childlessness and the disadvantages of parenthood.

Thus, 28 respondents were unable to cite even one disadvantage to being childless, even when this question was approached differently in an attempt to probe later in the interview. Most felt that there were no disadvantages to *their* being childless, given their life preferences. The following two comments are typical of others in the study:

> I can't really think of any disadvantages. It's a decision you have to make on your own because it's what you really want; it's best for you, not because you do it to save society or to please others [couple #21, wife].

> In my personal life, no, I can see no disadvantages to being childless. I don't see children as a bond that brings two people together. What Judy and I have could not be enhanced to any degree by children. If anything, it might be undermined because of the time that could not be devoted to each other. I don't think in later years I will be lonely because I don't have kids. I will be just as lonely as I want to be. I'll just build my relationships more with my peers and rely less on family relationships [couple #19, husband].

Respondents seemed to indicate, as can be seen in the comments above, that the decision to remain childless is a couple decision, rather than an individual decision, which is made as a result of an examination of the benefits of remaining childless. Such an examination does not appear to be made at any one particular point in time, but rather, the benefits are reviewed by the couple throughout the decision-making process until such time as the couple reaches an irrevocable or strong commitment. Costs, or disadvantages associated with being voluntarily childless are not as carefully weighed. Many couples have not even considered possible costs to themselves when they made this decision; the benefits of remaining childless were such as to preclude a thorough consideration of possible costs. Couples find the childless state is rewarding; the addition of children apparently is considered to be detrimental for personal and marital satisfaction.

CONCLUSIONS AND SUGGESTIONS
FOR FUTURE RESEARCH

This study has been concerned with the exploration of one particular variant family form: voluntarily childfree couples. Of particular interest have been the variables that may be associated with the decision not to have children and the process of decision making for such couples. We would like to reiterate two major findings and stress their implications, not only for future research on childless couples, but for family studies in general. First, the couple must be treated as a unit of analysis; and second, it is important to study the family *as process* as well as *as structure*.

THE COUPLE AS A UNIT OF ANALYSIS

Safilios-Rothschild (1969) has observed that much "family sociology" has been in fact "wives' family sociology." Due to the general availability of women as respondents, and perhaps the greater willingness and ability of wives to serve as interviewees in family studies, husbands have only infrequently been studied. In order to remedy this situation, some researchers (for example, Scanzoni, 1970) who have appreciated the weakness of wife-only research have begun to include both husbands and wives in their studies. Such efforts, however, usually do not include husbands and wives *married to each other*. While this is an improvement over wife-only sociology, it seems important not only to deal with both men's and women's respective perceptions, but also to treat the couple as a dyadic unit. This, of course, requires data from men and women married to each other.

Wife-only responses have contributed to the neglect of the husband-father role in sociological literature. It appears, however, that the primary task of the husband and father is that of being a breadwinner while the wife is the expressive family member responsible for the care of home and hearth. At least for middle-class professional males, the husband-father role is best filled through success in the occupational world. As Bell (1971: 328) observes:

> The fact that a man spends many hours away from home in his occupational role has a number of implications for his family. It seems probable that many upper middle-class males strongly identify with and for the most enjoy their professions. This kind of job involvement and satisfaction is generally not as characteristic of lower-class males.

In a simple summary statement, it might be asserted that the parental role is peripheral for the American middle-class husband. (For further discussions see LeMasters, 1974: 124-138; Young, 1973: 62-74; Bell, 1971: 323-327 and Benson, 1968.) Yet such assertions in the literature are not sufficient reason to omit the study of husbands in either research on marriage or parenthood. This study has attempted to analyze repsonses from both husbands and wives, primarily treating the couple when possible, rather than the individual as the unit of analysis. From the present data, it appears that the decision to parent or not to parent is one that is made by the couple and for the couple.

As we have seen, wives appear more likely than husbands to have made a personal commitment to a childfree life. While they acknowledge that the support of their spouses is essential, they seem to desire to remain childless, not only in their present marriages, but also, in the event of death or divorce, in any future marriage. Husbands, on the other hand, appear to be less personally committed to such a decision. A childfree life is desirable and satisfying in this marriage, but this decision would not necessarily carry over into another couple relationship. As one young husband expressed it:

> I'm not going to rule out anything. Let's say Sally were to die. If I met a woman with children who was widowed or divorced, that would not preclude me from marrying her. Nor would a woman's feeling that she wanted a family. If that was definitely what she wanted, it would be all right with me.

Both husbands and wives recognized that at the present time in our society, the bulk of childrearing responsibilities rests with women. Given this situation, the wives frequently acknowledged a greater "say" in the decision to remain childfree. The following quote from a 26-year-old social worker is typical of comments made by other wives:

> I am more committed to not having children than Marty is. I know I am not willing to give up my job or career—whatever you want to call it—to devote myself to being a full-time wife and mother; I don't think I could handle both motherhood and a career. I like my freedom; I like to be able to pick up and go and do pretty much what I want to and when I want to do it. I'm not sure I am willing to make the sacrifices and face the responsibilities of parenthood.

Based on our data several points become apparent regarding the husband's role in the couple's decision not to have children. First, the husband frequently is aware of the peripheral role and duties of "father" in American society, with the heaviest daily responsibility for childrearing falling to the wife-mother. Second, because of this awareness, the husband who is childfree is willing to support his wife in her desire not to have children. Third, although ruling out fatherhood for the present marital relationship, often men could envision themselves as fathers if they were married to women who desired children. (Wives were committed to their childfree life both as individuals and within a couple relationship. They were unable to perceive themselves as possibly marrying another man who wanted children.)

While undoubtedly there are couples where the husband has a stronger desire not to have children than does his wife, we did not have any such cases in our small sample. One reason may have been due to our research design, which required interviews with both husbands and wives. (We did have two refusals where the husband initially agreed to participate but backed down after consulting with his spouse.) Where the decision-making process is a source of tension in the marriage, participation in such a study is less likely than where the spouses are in agreement. Another reason why we may have not found husbands who were strongly committed to non-parenthood while the wives were not may be due to the female's control over most contraceptives. The old soap opera routine of a wife "accidentally" becoming pregnant and presenting her reluctant husband with an infant that captures his heart may be a plot in real life as on TV. Within our present sample, however, the husbands assumed a strongly supportive role while the wives could be said to be the main decision makers in remaining childfree.

DECISION-MAKING AS A PROCESS

Few of our couples decided on a childfree lifestyle before marriage. As we have seen, the majority of them assumed that at some point in the future they would become parents. There is evidence that in most cases the decision not to parent was a gradual one going through different stages.

The typical couple in our sample may have begun marriage thinking about having children "when the time was right," and some even going so far as to select names for future offspring. (Other couples, however, went no further than to assume they would have children.) At some time during the marriage, the couple recognized that a childfree life was a very satisfying one for them. They began to consider the alternative family form of remaining permanently childless. Some couples in this sample apparently have not completed the decision-making process. Although leaning toward remaining permanently childless, the couples who are "committed with reservations" are still not ready to consider sterilization due to a possible mind change. The "reasonably committed," although more resolute than the "committed with reservations," are not as resolved as the "strongly committed." The latter group appears to be the most likely candidates for sterilization, thus making an irrevocable commitment to their decision.

Not all couples, of course, go through all of these stages. Nor is any approximate time-length apparent for remaining in any stage. Some few couples decided to remain childless prior to marriage; others decided within the first year of marriage; still others took nearly a decade to reach this decision. What is apparent, however, is that, when couples profess to being voluntarily childfree, they may be anywhere along the path toward permanent commitment.

Ideally, more efforts in family sociology should utilize a longitudinal research design. The actual decision-making process for couples in this study is lost in time; only selectively perceived facts are recalled. The stages presented here, therefore, are only approximations and suggest the need for future research on this topic.

IMPLICATIONS FOR FUTURE RESEARCH

This small nonrandom sample of 30 midwestern couples—who professed to be voluntarily and permanently childfree at the time of initial contact—can do no more than suggest hypotheses to be tested on a larger, more representative sample. We would like to advance the following propositions for further research.

(1) The degree of the wife's resolve not to have children varies with her satisfaction with her job performance. As has been discussed elsewhere (Poloma and Garland, 1971), a career and career satisfaction is not a sufficient cause for choosing a childfree life—but it may be a necessary one. Only one woman in our sample was unemployed and only one additional one has only part-time employment. While many women reported that they were job rather than career oriented, all did enjoy working. Some reported that the only condition under which they could imagine having a child is if they lost their jobs and were no longer productive members of society.

(2) The degree of the couple's resolve not to have children is contingent upon the wife's ability to make the decision and the husband's ability and willingness to support it. Most wives in our sample were admittedly more resolute in their decision to remain childfree than were the husbands. Wives viewed their decision as both personally important and important to the marital relationship. Husbands were more likely to perceive childlessness as being important to the present marital relationship but not necessarily relevant to a subsequent hypothetical relationship in the event of divorce or spouse's death.

(3) The couple's degree of resolve not to have children is contingent in the early stages of the decision-making process upon either full support of the parents or upon a distant relationship with the parents. Most of the couples in our sample reported a satisfactory relationship with both sets of

parents, but there was usually not a close interaction pattern. Most couples lived at least 30 miles away from both sets of parents. Some couples observed that this was important during the early stages of decision-making. A couple who visits their parents once or twice a year has less opportunity to experience parental pressure to have children than a couple who frequently interacts with the parents.

(4) The resolve not to have children is contingent upon an awareness of the existence of the phenomenon but not upon close contact with like-minded couples. Most couples in our sample knew of other childless couples and many had read a magazine article or seen a TV program on the phenomenon. Only two couples were members of NON (National Organization of Non-Parents) and most did not see a need for such an organization for themselves. Their close friends may have children or to be planning to have them. Parental status did not appear to negate the possibility of friendship with other couples. In fact support often comes from friends who are parents who admit that "parenthood is not all that it's cracked up to be."

(5) The decision not to have children is a process that may be modified over time; it may begin with a desire to have children, followed by doubts about the desirability of parenthood, and finally culminating in a resolute decision. The decision not to have children was reached by only four couples before marriage. For the most part it was a gradual process fed by a general satisfaction with life the way it was—without children. Simple chance, particularly in the form of contraceptive success, seems to play a role in whether the couple continues in the route toward a resolute decision not to have children or whether they become parents. Marginally committed couples are the most likely to become parents as a result of an unplanned pregnancy.

(6) Perceived ability to assume parental roles varies with the degree of commitment. The stronger the commitment, the less the ability to view oneself as a "good parent." Most couples who were strongly committed to remaining childless were free in admitting their perceived inability to deal with children of some or all age groups. (For example, an elementary school teacher may express a liking for young children but a dislike for adolescents.) Many women admitted to atypical sibling experiences of either no siblings or of many siblings. In the latter case, some wives discussed their role as mother substitute for their younger siblings—a role that was not to their liking.

(7) Strained relations with one or both parents while growing up adds further cognitive support for a perceived inability to execute parental roles successfully. While it probably cannot be asserted that strained parental relations causes a decision not to have children, it may be used as a source of cognitive support by both husbands and wives. Being so close to someone who was not an "ideal parent" feeds into the recognition that not all people should be parents.

The above are suggested hypotheses for testing within a sample of voluntarily childfree couples. The data also suggest some hypotheses to be tested on a sample of childfree couples and a matched sample of parents.

(1) Wives are the key decision makers in the decision to have children. While the role of *parent* applies to both fathers and mothers, it is the mother who assumes primary responsibility for child-care. This reason was given by many of the husbands in our sample, in indicating that any change in their childless status would have to be one initiated by their wives. It appears that much more emphasis is placed on socializing girls to accept the role of mother than on boys to accept the father role. We are suggesting that middle-class men are more flexible in making a decision to parent than are middle-class women.

(2) Couples who are childfree are less likely to express a religious preference or a strong religious attachment than those with children. Established religions have tended to support the existing structural arrangements, including the view that marriage implies at least desiring parenthood. In fact, a prenuptial agreement not to have children on the part of the couple is an impediment to a Catholic marriage. While other churches may be less legalistic, it is probable that they reflect the culutral norm to have children.

The relationship between church preference and parenthood may be two-fold. First, voluntarily childfree couples are breaking a cultural norm in deciding not to parent. Established religions would do little to support them in this decision and may actually serve as agents exerting "pressure" to modify the decision. Second, parents may be reluctant to abandon church affiliation for "the sake of the children."

(3) Childfree couples are more likely to be oriented to the husband-wife relationship than the parents. Our data suggest that childless couples are very conscious of the quality of their marital relationships. For both husbands and wives, the spouse is the most significant other. When and if

this situation ceases, the marital relationship is in jeopardy. As Simmel (1950: 123) has observed in discussing the difference between a dyad and a triad:

> This dependence of the dyad upon its two individual members causes the thought of its existence to be accompanied by the thought of the termination much more closely and impressively than in any other group, where every member knows that even after his retirement or death, the group can continue to exist.

Parents have the option of viewing either the spouse-role or the parent-role as their cardinal role. For childfree couples the marital relationship is of primary importance.

(4) Husbands in childfree couples are less likely to perceive themselves as breadwinners and "main earners" within the family than are fathers. The husbands in our sample were unlikely to perceive themselves as breadwinners. In most cases, the wives were also employed, making responsibility for the couples' finances a joint venture. With the advent of woman's liberation, it is less popular to conceive of the husband as "taking care of" his wife. The father, however, must assume that role in relation to his child. It is assumed that it is his responsibility to meet the family's financial needs, even when the wife is employed.

(5) Couples in which the husband alone can assume full responsibility for maintaining the family's desired standard of living are more likely to have children than those where both husband's and wife's full-time income is required. In a study conducted on dual-career families (Poloma and Garland, 1971), it was observed that almost all couples studied wanted and had children. The average income of these high-status professional couples was significantly greater than that of this sample of childfree couples. We wish to suggest that the higher the income the easier it is to combine parenthood and two careers. The childfree couples in this sample required the income of both spouses to maintain their desired living standard.

(6) Childfree couples perceive greater marital satisfaction than do parental couples. The relationship between the presence of children and marital happiness is far from clear. Bernard (1972: 60-63) reports that childless couples perceive greater marital satisfaction, but Campbell's (1975) study does not completely support this contention. A matched sample may enable researchers to determine whether there is a relationship between parenthood and marital satisfaction.

These hypotheses are not meant to exhaust the proposition in need of research. Rather they suggest points for consideration that have been gleaned in this exploratory project and ones in need of further study.

REFERENCES

BALCHIN, N. (1965) "Children are a waste of time." Saturday Evening Post 9 (October): 10-11.
BELL, R. R. (1971) Marriage and Family Interaction (third ed.) Homewood, Ill.: Dorsey.
BENSON, L. (1968) Fatherhood: A Sociological Perspective. New York: Random House.
BERNARD, J. (1972) The Future of Marriage. New York: Bantam.
BLOOD, R. O. and D. M. WOLFE (1972) Husbands and Wives: The Dynamics of Married Living. New York: Free Press.
CAMPBELL, A. (1975) "The American way of mating: marriage si, children only maybe." Psychology Today (May): 37-41.
DUVALL, E. M. (1971) Family Development (fourth ed.) Philadelphia: Lippincott.
FREEDMAN, R., P. K. WHELPTON, and A. A. CAMPBELL (1969) Family Planning, Sterility, and Population Growth. New York: McGraw-Hill.
GRINDSTAFF, C. F. (1976) "Trends and incidence of childlessness by race: indicators of black progress over three decades." Sociological Focus (forthcoming).
GRABILL, W. and P. GLICK (1959) "Demographic and social aspects of childlessness: census data." Milbank Memorial Fund Q. 37: 60-86.
GREENE, G. (1963) "A vote against motherhood." Saturday Evening Post 236 (January): 10-12.
GUSTAVUS, S. O. and J. R. HENLEY, Jr. (1971) "Correlates of voluntary childlessness in a select population." Social Biology 18 (September): 277-284.
HOLLINGSHEAD, A. B. (1957) Two Factor Index of Social Position. (mimeo).
––– and F. C. REDLICH (1958) Social Class and Mental Illness: A Community Study. New York: Wiley.
HOOVER, W. and D. E. BENSON (1974) "The stigmatization of a deviant group: the case of voluntarily childless couples." Paper presented at North Central Soc. Assn. meetings (May).
KISER, C. V. (1939) "Voluntary and involuntary aspects of childlessness." Milbank Memorial Fund Q. 17: 50-68.
––– W. H. GRABILL, and A. A. CAMPBELL (1968) Trends and Variations in Fertility in the United States. Cambridge, Mass.: Harvard Univ. Press.
KUCZNSKI, R. R. (1938) "Childless marriages." Sociological Rev. 30: 120-144.
LeMASTERS, E. E. (1974) Parents in Modern America. Homewood, Ill.: Dorsey.
LESLIE, G. R. (1973) The Family in Social Context (second ed.). New York: Oxford Univ. Press.
LOPATA, H. Z. (1965) "The secondary features of a primary relationship." Human Organization 24: 116-123.
MARTINSON, F. M. (1970) Family in Society. New York: Dodd, Mead.

MICHELS, L. (1970) "Why we don't want children." Redbook Magazine (January): 10-14.

PECK, E. (1971) The Baby Trap. New York: Bernard Geiss Assn.

POHLMAN, E., J. FRUTH, J. GROSSMITH, D. PARRISH, S. FASKAN, and L. SABRAW (1971) "Changes in views toward intentional childlessness 1965-1970 among college students." Unpub. paper.

POLOMA, M. M. and T. N. GARLAND (1972) "On the social construction of reality: reported husband-wife differences." Sociological Focus 5 (Winter): 40-54.

––– (1971) "Cribs or careers? Professionally employed married women's attitudes toward motherhood." Paper presented at the Amer. Soc. Assn. meetings (August).

POPENOE, P. (1943) "Childlessness: voluntary or involuntary." J. of Heredity 34: 83-84.

––– (1936) "Motivation of childless marriages." J. of Heredity 27: 469-472.

RADL, S. L. (1973) Mother's Day is Over. New York: Charterhouse.

RAO, S.L.N. (1974) "A comparative study of childlessness and never-pregnant status." J. of Marriage and the Family 36 (February): 149-157.

RODGERS, R. H. (1973) Family Interaction and Transaction: The Developmental Approach. Englewood Cliffs, N.J.: Prentice-Hall.

SAFILIOS-ROTHSCHILD, C. (1969) "Family sociology or wives' family sociology? A cross-cultural examination of decision making." J. of Marriage and the Family 2 (May): 290-301.

SCANZONI, J. H. (1970) Opportunity and the Family. New York: Free Press.

SILVERMAN, A. and A. SILVERMAN (1971) The Case Against Having Children. New York: David McKay.

SIMMEL, G. (1950) The Sociology of Georg Simmel. Kurt H. Wolff [ed.] Glencoe, Ill.: Free Press.

SKLAR, J. (1971) "Childless women." Paper presented at annual meeting, Population Assn. of America (April).

U.S. Bureau of the Census (1973) Women by Number of Children Ever Born. Washington, D.C.: U.S. Gov. Print. Office.

VEEVERS, J. E. (1974a) "The lifestyle of voluntarily childless couples." In Lyle Larson [ed.] The Canadian Family in Comparative Perspective. Toronto: Prentice Hall.

––– (1974b) "The moral careers of voluntarily childless wives: notes on the defense of a variant world view." In S. Parvez Wakil [ed.] Marriage and the Family in Canada: A Reader. Toronto: Capp-Clark.

––– (1973) "The social meaning of parenthood." Psychiatry 36 (August): 291-310.

––– (1972) "The violation of fertility mores: voluntary childlessness as deviant behavior." In Grandstaff and Whitehead [ed.] Deviant Behaviour and Societal Reaction. Toronto: Holt, Rinehart & Winston.

––– (1971) "Childlessness and age at first marriage." Social Biology 18 (September): 292-295.

WHELPTON, P. K., A. A. CAMPBELL, and J. C. PATTERSON (1966) Fertility and Family Planing in the United States. Princeton, N.J.: Princeton Univ. Press.

YOUNG, L. (1973) The Fractured Family. New York: McGraw-Hill.

APPENDIX: BACKGROUND INFORMATION

Couple #	Age H	Age W	Educational Attainment H	Educational Attainment W	Religion Now H	Religion Now W	Religion Brought Up H	Religion Brought Up W	Occupation H	Occupation W	Income
1	22	21	HS	HS	Rom. Cath.	Rom. Cath.	Rom. Cath.	Rom. Cath.	Factory laborer	(Unemployed; clerical)	10,000
2	25	24	Some Grad. work	B.A.	None	Prot.	Prot.	Prot.	Counselor	Counselor	15,000
3	27	25	M.A.	B.A.	Prot.	Prot.	Prot.	Prot.	Social Worker	Counselor	15,000
4	30	26	Some Coll.	Some Coll.	Prot.	Prot.	Prot.	Prot.	Mortician	Secretary	20,000
5	28	26	B.A.	B.S.	Prot.	None	Prot.	Prot.	H.S. Teacher	Elem. Teacher	15,000
6	26	24	Some Grad. Work	B.A.	None	None	Prot.	Prot.	Grad. Stud.	Secretary	6,000
7	29	26	B.A.	M.A.	Prot.	Prot.	Prot.	Prot.	H.S. Teacher	H.S. Teacher	16,000
8	25	25	Some Grad. Work	Some Grad. Work	Prot.	None	Prot.	Prot.	Employment Counselor	Rental Agent	10,000
9	26	25	Some Grad. Work	Some Coll.	None	Rom. Cath.	Rom. Cath.	Rom. Cath.	Grad. Stud.	Coll. Stud.	10,000
10	26	26	M.A.	M.A.	Rom. Cath.	Rom. Cath.	Rom. Cath.	Rom. Cath.	Engineer	Grad. Stud.	17,000
11	29	25	B.A.	M.A.	Rom. Cath.	Rom. Cath.	Rom. Cath.	Rom. Cath.	Management	Research	12,000
12	29	28	B.A.	B.A.	Prot.	None	Prot.	Rom. Cath.	Advertising	Counselor	18,000

Couple #	Age H	Age W	Educational Attainment H	Educational Attainment W	Religion Now H	Religion Now W	Religion Brought Up H	Religion Brought Up W	Occupation H	Occupation W	Income
13	28	26	Law Deg.	Some Coll.	None	Jew	Rom. Cath.	Jew	CPA	Media Director	20,000+
14	28	21	B.A.	Some Coll.	Prot.	None	Prot.	Rom. Cath.	Creative Specialist	Advertising	20,000
15	29	28	B.S.	Some Coll.	None	None	Prot.	Prot.	Engineer	Secretary	22,000
16	35	36	Some Grad. Work	Some Grad. Work	None	None	Prot.	Prot.	Engineer	Artist	17,000
17	26	26	Some Coll.	Some Grad. Work	Prot.	Prot.	Prot.	Prot.	Auto mechanic	Librarian	16,000
18	29	26	Some Grad. Work	Some Coll.	None	None	Prot.	Rom. Cath.	Law Stud.	Secretary	6,000
19	29	27	M.S.	H.S.	None	Rom. Cath.	Rom. Cath.	Rom. Cath.	Accountant	Clerical Supervisor	20,000
20	26	24	B.A.	B.A.	Prot.	Prot.	Prot.	Prot.	Engineer	Computer Programmer	18,000
21	26	22	M.A.	M.A.	None	Prot.	None	Prot.	H.S. Teacher	Grad. Stud.	12,000
22	36	45	Some Coll.	M.A.	None	None	Prot.	Rom. Cath.	Salesman	Training Director	17,000
23	28	26	Some Grad. Work	B.A.	Prot.	None	Prot.	None	Engineer	Social Work	25,000
24	26	25	B.A.	B.A.	None	Rom. Cath.	Rom. Cath.	Rom. Cath.	Journalist	Journalist	26,000

APPENDIX – Continued

Couple #	Age H	Age W	Educational Attainment H	Educational Attainment W	Religion Now H	Religion Now W	Religion Brought Up H	Religion Brought Up W	Occupation H	Occupation W	Income
25	30	30	H.S.	H.S.	Rom. Cath.	Rom. Cath.	Rom. Cath.	Prot.	Car Lot Manager	Unemployed	28,000
26	26	26	B.S.	B.A.	None	None	Prot.	Prot.	Salesman	Social Work	11,000
27	32	26	Ph.D.	M.A.	Rom. Cath.	Rom. Cath.	Prot.	Rom. Cath.	Professor	Journalist	25,000
28	31	25	Some Grad. Work	B.A.	None	None	Rom. Cath.	Rom. Cath.	Underwriter	H.S. Teacher	18,000
29	31	26	Some Coll.	Some Grad. Work	None	None	Prot.	Prot.	Photographer	Grad. Stud.	10,000
30	26	24	B.A.	Some Coll.	None	None	Prot.	Prot.	Book Salesman	Public Relations	19,000

APPENDIX – Continued

Couple #	Number of Siblings H	Number of Siblings W	Number of Younger Siblings H	Number of Younger Siblings W	Number of Organizations Belong H	Number of Organizations Belong W	Number of Organizations Active H	Number of Organizations Active W	Rent or Own	Yrs. Married
1	1	4	1	1	1	None	None	None	Rent	1.0
2	1	2	None	None	1	5	1	3	Rent	3.0
3	3	8	2	4	None	3	2	3	Rent	5.5
4	None	4	None	4	2	2	2	2	Own	6.0
5	None	7	None	7	4	3	2	3	Own	6.5
6	4	3	2	3	None	3	None	3	Rent	4.0
7	2	None	None	None	3	1	None	1	Rent	4.0
8	1	3	1	3	2	3	None	None	Rent	4.0
9	4	3	4	3	None	None	None	None	Rent	4.0
10	7	4	6	1	2	2	None	None	Rent	6.0
11	2	2	1	2	None	1	None	1	Own	3.0
12	1	1	1	1	None	1	9	2	Rent	5.0
13	2	1	1	1	10	6	None	1	Rent	5.0
14	None	2	None	2	None	1	2	2	Rent	2.5
15	None	2	None	1	None	3	None	1	Rent	5.0
16	2	None	2	None	3	3	None	1	Own	13.0
17	4	3	3	3	1	4	None	1	Rent	7.0
18	1	1	1	1	None	2	None	1	Rent	5.0
19	1	2	None	None	1	1	None	None	Rent	8.0
20	2	2	1	2	None	5	None	1	Rent	3.5
21	1	1	None	None	None	5	None	2	Rent	3.0
22	2	3	2	1	5	None	None	None	Own	5.0
23	2	None	2	None	2	3	1	1	Rent	4.5
24	5	5	5	5	None	None	None	None	Rent	4.0
25	3	1	1	None	None	None	None	None	Own	8.0
26	4	4	4	2	5	6	1	5	Rent	6.0
27	2	5	2	5	1	None	None	None	Rent	4.0
28	3	1	2	1	None	1	None	None	Rent	2.0
29	1	1	1	1	None	1	None	None	Rent	7.0
30	2	3	2	3	None	5	None	2	Own	5.0

ELLEN MARA NASON is an instructor at Sinclair Community College. She received her M.A. in sociology from the University of Akron.

MARGARET M. POLOMA is presently an associate professor of sociology at the University of Akron. She received her Ph.D. in sociology from Case Western Reserve University. Author of a number of articles dealing with the dual-career family, she is currently a coauthor of the quarterly scholarly journal Sociological Focus.